# Kingdom Revelation

Burton S. Sherbert

# KINGDOM REVELATION

Burton S. Sherbert

© 2017 Burton S. Sherbert
**KINGDOM REVELATION**

Cover photo by Harrod Publishing
Edited by Tracy Morgan

Unless otherwise identified, Scripture quotations are from the HOLY BIBLE, NEW INTERNATIONAL VERSION ®, Copyright © 173, 178, 194 by International Bible Society Used by permission of Zondervan Publishing House. All rights reserved. Scripture quotations identified KJV are from the King James Version of the Bible.

All rights reserved. No part of this publication may be reproduced, stored in a retrieval system, or transmitted in any form or by any means -- electronic, mechanical, photocopying, recording, or otherwise -- without the prior written permission of author or publisher.

Published by Harrod Publishing
www.harrodpublishing.com
(240) 303-8062

Printed in the United States
Library of Congress
Harrod Enterprises LLC

---

**KINGDOM REVELATION**
BURTON S. SHERBERT

ISBN-10:  0-9988809-0-6
ISBN-13:  978-0-9988809-0-7

## Dedication

I want to dedicate this book to the memory of my Grandmother the Late Missionary Ella B. Wallace. I am doing what you and Mom raised me to do. I love you and miss you so much!

## Acknowledgments

There are too many people to thank for the inspiration of this book but I would like to thank my Lord and Savior for without Him I would be nothing.

I want to thank my Mom, Elder Connie B. Stewart. Thank You for everything that you have done for me and for always seeing the best in me! Thank You Dad (David Stewart, Sr.) for always being there. My biological brother David, Jr. You are MY hero and my closest friend; thank you for loving me.

To the Greatest Assistant Pastor anyone could ask for Elder Rudolph Brooks, Jr. Thank you for your continued support.

To my amazing Executive Administrator, Minister Levonne Wiseman. There are no words to describe how the Lord has used you with me.

To my Apostolic Father, Bishop Michael D. Densmore & Lady Stacey Densmore. Thank You for speaking life into me!

Special Thanks to my entire church family Kingdom Tabernacle of Refuge Ministries, Inc.

## THE BEGINNING

I began writing this book about three years, ago not realizing there was more to be revealed! When I began writing this book, I thought I was just going to discuss the Kingdom as it pertains to revelation and what that meant; however, I learned that Kingdom Revelation is something that cannot be explained. It must be experienced. Kingdom was revealed to me, but I also had an opportunity to experience it firsthand.

When I began this journey into the Kingdom, it was revealed to me that I had access to heavenly provision, but here is the catch: You can only be a testimony to "Kingdom provision" if you have been in a situation where you needed "Kingdom provisions." I have witnessed God giving me ministry provisions when there was none. This all began with the prophetic word that "the success of my ministry was going to be the visibility of my ministry." I knew exactly what that meant.

I only shared this with one person . . . On a daily basis; I would drive by a building in Upper Marlboro, Maryland. The building was in the perfect location – right smack in the middle of the of the DMV area. It had gold bricks, ample parking and the perfect structure for a church. The door was open. This building had been vacant for about five years. It was an open space with tremendous potential. I did not know all that needed to be done for my vision to come to pass, but I was ecstatic! My church shared in my excitement . . . the excitement of finally having a building we could be proud of.

In the meantime, we were worshiping in the basement of an old facility that was once a jail in Anne Arundel County. During the winter months, we had no heat; and in the summer months, we melted because we did not have air conditioning; but because of our love for God, we made it work. Although we made it work, there was some undercurrent talk among the people about the building's conditions. Like any other Pastor, after a while that kind of talk wears on you. People may say they understand how you feel, but until you are a Pastor who is responsible for making decisions that will cause either success or failure, you will never understand. It is so important for you to pray for your Pastor! Pray for his or her mind, clarity, and focus because once that is gone; it is difficult to get it back.

By faith, we stepped out of the boat and placed a security deposit on the building. We left the basement in Anne Arundel County with nowhere to go. For a few Sundays, we held services in the building we were constructing, but the condition of that building was not conducive for those services. There was so much dust and mold in the building. It just was not healthy. I began receiving reports that the saints were getting sick, so we searched for and found a church to rent. For the time being, the church worked and it was just what we needed at that time. We held services and it was good.

As time went on, we hired an architect and an engineer to design the layout of our building. We spent money before even one nail was banged into the walls. There were strict county codes, so it was important that proper building permits be in place before the work could begin, otherwise, the inspectors would shut our project right on down. When the architect and the engineers finished with the plans, it took one year to get the plans approved by the county. For an entire year, the building we were so excited about sat untouched because of the laws in Prince George's County.

The plans were approved after one full year and to my surprise, we encountered another obstacle: The majority of the faithful tithers left. Over the years people left, but I had never been as affected by any group's leaving as I had by this particular one. I felt I had failed at what God called me to do.

## A TRANSPARENT MOMENT

Although I was up preaching, jumping, and shouting, my inward man was quite disappointed and depressed. I did not understand why I was going through what I was going through. I had experienced profound betrayals from those close to me. That season was so disappointing to me. Oftentimes, people were having meetings about me in their houses. I really had to pray and ask the Lord to veil my heart because I did not want become bitter with His people. It is very easy to sit back and judge a man or woman of God until you experience what life feels like to walk in their shoes.

Kingdom Provision, in this scenario, was *"You will guard him and keep him in perfect and constant peace whose mind [both its inclination and its character] is stayed on You, because he commits himself to You, leans on You, and hopes confidently in You. So trust in the Lord (commit yourself to Him, lean on Him, hope confidently in Him) forever; for the Lord God is an everlasting Rock [the Rock of Ages]* (Isaiah 26:3-4 AMPC).

I experienced the Word of God becoming flesh for me. It is because of Him that I was kept in my right mind. There were times when I did not feel anyone was in my corner. Yes, my mother, brother, and others in my church proved they loved and respected by saying things like, "Pastor, we don't care where we have service; we're going to be right there." They kept their word and stood by my side. I believe we would have given up had the Lord not been with us.

**P**salm 124 (AMP) Praise for Rescue from Enemies

*A Song of [a]Ascents. Of David. "If it had not been the* LORD *who was on our side," Let Israel now say, ² "If it had not been the* LORD *who was on our side When men rose up against us, ³ Then they would have [quickly] swallowed us alive, When their wrath was kindled against us; ⁴ Then the waters would have engulfed us, The torrent would have swept over our soul;⁵ Then the [b]raging waters would have swept over our soul." ⁶ Blessed be the LORD, Who has not given us as prey to be torn by their teeth. ⁷ We have escaped like a bird from the snare of the fowlers; The trap is broken and we have escaped. ⁸ Our help is in the name of the LORD, Who made heaven and earth.*

We moved from one building to the next and with each move, problems followed us. It seemed as if this was going to be my life's story and ministry. We were confronted with a mighty warfare. There was always a financial need, and we were often left with more bills than money. Our budget did not match our income. We finally secured a facility in the vicinity of our future building. God blessed us to be able to stay there, comfortably. for two years. Of course, when you're sharing a space, there will always be problems, but it started out well.

Once we began sharing this space, we also began rebuilding and growing our ministry. The Lord's blessing was upon us. We were fellowshipping in an historical building right in the heart of Upper Marlboro, Maryland and we were being blessed.

The historical building and its upkeep began taking its toll on us. The utilities went up and there was "wear and tear" damage to the building. Can you imagine what it feels like to wonder "When is the last ball going to drop?" every time you walk into a place? Please keep in mind that during this time, not only were we paying rent in this historical building, but we were also paying contractors and buying materials.

In the space of about three years, we were asked to leave the historical building where we were having our services because it was taking too long to complete the construction of our new building. By this time, we had invested $50,000 into this space. I was absolutely, completely devastated! Everything within me wanted to die and give up! Nevertheless, because of my "Revelation," I knew giving up was not an option.

I received both letters indicating that we were no longer able to occupy the space. The building that we were building out canceled our contract and the church that we were renting also terminated our contract in the same week, and on top of that, I was headed to California to preach a three-day revival. I was not able to break down like I really wanted to. In my gut, I knew things were going to come together because of what had been revealed! When you get a revelation from the Lord, it does not matter what comes up against that revelation; what's *Revealed* is *Sealed*! I had choices: I could have done what I knew to do and taken them to court, or I could have waited on God for an answer. The Spirit of the Lord said to me, "Let it go!" I took my Isaac, which was the building I wanted so badly, and I trusted God to make everything all right. Right at that moment, I received Kingdom Provision.

In a matter of two weeks, I watched manna fall straight from heaven. The Lord opened up another door that was better than the door to the historical building. When that door opened, we had the money to go in by a miraculous "Kingdom Provision." Whatever God has revealed, HEAVEN has sealed. Moreover, it happened just like God said it would!

During those times of uncertainty, I had to call forth the Word of God!

*"Do not, therefore, fling away your fearless confidence, for it carries a great and glorious compensation of reward. For you have need of steadfast patience and endurance, so that you may perform and fully accomplish the will of God, and thus receive and carry away [and enjoy to the full] what is promised. For still a little while (a very little while), and the Coming One will come and He will not delay, But the just shall live by faith [My righteous servant shall live by his conviction respecting man's relationship to God and divine things, and holy fervor born of faith and conjoined with it]: and if he draws back and shrinks in*

*fear, My soul has no delight or pleasure in him"* (Hebrews 10:35-38, AMPC).

*"And the Lord answered me and said, Write the vision and engrave it so plainly upon tablets that everyone who passes may [be able to] read [it easily and quickly] as he hastens by. For the vision is yet for an appointed time and it hastens to the end [fulfillment]; it will not deceive or disappoint. Though it tarry, wait [earnestly] for it, because it will surely come; it will not be behindhand on its appointed day"* (Habakkuk 2:2-3, AMPC)

As you read this book, my prayer is that you will open up your spirit and reflect upon any situation you are dealing with. Think about the times you have seen Kingdom Provisions at work. There will be times when no one will be able to help you. As a Kingdom Citizen, you must report to the Embassy of the Kingdom of God. You have direct access to His provision, intelligence, wisdom and ideals. There is no need to walk in fear of any impending situation. Stand still and see the salvation of the Lord. Remember, *"What God has revealed, heaven has sealed!*

## KINGDOM REVELATION

When we understand that Kingdom is a mindset and a privilege from the King, it will change the way we think, act, and speak. Kingdom Revelation is information that comes directly from the Father in heaven. So when trouble comes to discourage you, you don't have to become shaken or dismayed because you have the inside scoop on what The Father has said about you. Kingdom represents dominion. This simply means we are in position to reign and rule on earth as it is in heaven.

The book of Genesis tells us that God created man in His image (Genesis 1:27). God created us in His image so we would take on His Image and His likeness – that means we have the character and the works of God! When we receive this as *Rhema*, it should immediately transform our minds to another level of confidence and faith in God. We will realize that God created us to duplicate His works! Jesus spoke to us from the Word and said *"Greater works than these shall ye do in my name;"* unfortunately, we do not have enough revelation of that text to be able to comprehend "Greater!"

It takes greater faith in God and His Word to operate and function in Kingdom Revelation! Although those are two different words in the Kingdom "Image and Likeness" we can use them interchangeably. We find that in John 1, God is His Word and the Word is God. You cannot separate the two and expect to function in Kingdom Revelation. When one has Kingdom Revelation, it means one is entirely convinced of his or her position and relationship with God. You cannot function in Kingdom business without having a real relationship with God.

Revelation is derived from a connection with the Father that few people have reached. The Bible tells us in Mark 4:11, *"And he said to them, to you have been entrusted the mystery of the Kingdom of God [that is the secret counsels of God which are hidden from the ungodly; but for those outside [of our circle] everything becomes a parable."(amp)*

Jesus was very clear when He stated that the kingdom of God was a mystery. You cannot function in anything you cannot comprehend. If the Father has not given you revelation, you are not in a relationship with Him. The Kingdom of God is not something that can be taught or figured out; it must be revealed through personal time with the Father.

The word "revelation" comes from the Greek word "Apocalypto" or "Apocalypse" which means to be unveiled.

When we are without revelation, we have spiritual blinders on with no foresight or insight. On the other hand, Kingdom Revelation reaches far beyond your five senses: touching, hearing, tasting, smelling or seeing. Kingdom Revelation is outside of the realm of your senses. When you understand the mystery of the Kingdom, you do not need a sign from God because you already know the outcome.

When we have Kingdom Revelation, we do not have to rely on the world's sources because the Kingdom has already made provision for us in the earth (Matthew 6:10 - Thy kingdom come, Thy will be done on earth as it is in heaven.). The Kingdom is more than just a place or space. It is a realm that one can tap into on earth. In truth, we are Kingdom citizens living temporarily on earth.

When we understand we are ambassadors of the Kingdom, we realize that our mindsets are not locked into this world's system, but into the systematic principles of the Kingdom. For example, if I go to another country to work for the United States of America, I am not bound by foreign laws; I am functioning in another country the same way I function in my native land. When we operate as Kingdom citizens while on earth, we qualify for the diplomatic privileges granted by the Kingdom of God.

I have an assignment that must be carried out in the earth. My accountability is not to those in the earth, but to those who are of the same citizenship. While on an assignment in another country, if you encounter any issues, you are expected to take those issues to your embassy in that particular country. It is the same way in the Kingdom of God. If you encounter any issues while on earth, if anything comes up that you cannot handle, you always have access to the Kingdom Embassy of God! This, again, is a state of mind. Once you begin to think it, you can walk in it and see results! Doors that were shut will start to open up once you adopt this mindset of Kingdom Revelation.

When Kingdom is revealed to you, things about yourself are also revealed. When you operate in Kingdom revelation, it is very hard for you to be convinced of anything contrary to what God has revealed.

The word "diplomat" is defined as a person who represents his or her country's government in a foreign country; Someone whose work is diplomacy, an individual who has skills in dealing with other people (Merriam-Webster).

As a diplomat of the Kingdom, God has given us Kingdom skill in dealing with individuals in the earth, so Kingdom power draws a significant level of favor. Proverbs 3:4 (AMPC) discusses favor: *"So shall you find favor, good understanding, and high esteem in the sight (or judgment) of God and man.* It is paramount that in all our getting, we must get an understanding that comes from God, the Father. The Bible says, in Proverbs chapter four and verse seven, *"The beginning of Wisdom is: get Wisdom (skillful and godly Wisdom)! [For skillful and godly Wisdom is the principal thing.] And with all you have gotten, get understanding (discernment, comprehension, and interpretation).* When you are in Kingdom and you function in Kingdom, you have a keen understanding of who you are and who God is. That kind of understanding can only come by revelation. Many Christians know how to function in the tradition of who they have been in God, but few know how to operate in the Kingdom.

The Apostle Paul stated: *[After all] the kingdom of God is not a matter of [getting the] food and drink [one likes], but instead, it is righteousness (that state which makes a person acceptable to God) and [heart] peace and joy in the Holy Spirit"* (Romans 14:17, AMPC). The Kingdom of God is not what we have made it. The Kingdom of God is righteousness, peace, and joy. It is something we can experience "on earth as it is in heaven." Worldly wisdom cannot obtain this; it must be obtained through the Spirit of God.

## WHAT IS REVELATION?

Revelation is an act of revealing or communication of divine truth: something that is revealed by God to humans: an act of revealing to view or making known: something that is revealed; especially: an enlightening or astonishing disclosure.

If something is revealed, it means that before it was revealed – it was hidden.

The Prophet Isaiah prophesied: "And I will give you the treasures of darkness and hidden riches of secret places, that you may know that it is I, the Lord, the God of Israel, Who calls you by your name" Isaiah 45:3 (AMPC). In this text, God was speaking through Isaiah, letting His people know He had blessings in store for them that they were not even aware of. There are certain plans and purposes God has in store for us that have yet to be revealed. The Apostle Paul said it this way in I Corinthians 13:9-12 (AMPC): *"For our knowledge is fragmentary (incomplete and imperfect), and our prophecy (our teaching) is fragmentary (incomplete and imperfect). But when the complete and perfect (total) comes, the incomplete and perfect will vanish away (become antiquated, void, and superseded). When I was a child, I talked like a child, I thought like a child, I reasoned like a child; now that I have become a man, I am done with childish ways and have put them aside. For now we are looking in a mirror that gives only a dim (blurred) reflection [of reality as in a riddle or enigma], but then [when perfection comes] we shall see in reality and face to face! Now I know in part (imperfectly), but then I shall know and understand fully and clearly, even in the same manner as I have been fully and clearly known and understood [by God].*

The Apostle Paul was teaching the church at Corinth that although we prophesy divine truths, we do not know God's complete plan for our lives. The more we walk in relationship with God, the more He reveals to us. Although we have knowledge and understanding of who God is, there is still a lot about the Father we do not know. Yes, we may have an idea or a concept about our life or our purpose, but there are still things God has in store for us that we have not tapped into yet.

Revelation is the thing we can see about ourselves or someone else that can only be seen in the Spirit. Revelation comes through the Holy Spirit. We must understand that when God has a specific assignment for our lives, there are secret things He must share with us that others will not be able to understand. In the previous chapter, I mentioned Mark 4:11 (AMPC): *"And He said to them, To you has been entrusted the mystery of the kingdom of God [that is, the secret counsels of God which are hidden from the ungodly]; but for those outside [of our circle] everything becomes a parable."* Let us really look at this text. Jesus shared this information with His disciples, the ones He trusted to pour into for a specific work. His trust in them meant they were called, anointed, and appointed by God to work for the Kingdom of God. In using these men, Jesus had to share the mystery of the kingdom of God with them –the secret counsels of God which are HIDDEN from the ungodly.

The only way the ungodly will understand the mystery of the kingdom of God is if it is revealed. The Kingdom of God will not be revealed to someone who does not possess Kingdom citizenship. Certain things cannot be shared with certain people who are not of the same fold. It is important to know this is both a law and a principle. *For example*: Let us consider a person who has a high security clearance in the government. That person must take an oath promising to keep certain things about their job and duties of their job confidential. It is the same way when you have a major assignment in the kingdom of God. You cannot go around sharing everything the Lord has revealed to you.

The Bible very clearly states, in the book of Matthew: *"But when you give to charity do not let your left hand know what your right hand is doing"* (Matthew 6:13, AMPC). There are things that must be kept silent. Revelation is something to be appreciated and honored because few people find it.

Matthew, the seventh chapter and fourteenth verse says, *"But the gate is narrow (contracted by pressure and the way is straitened and compressed that leads away to life, and few are those who find it"* (AMPC). It's important to understand that Revelation is given to those that have a great purpose and is not to be taken lightly. Revelation sets you apart from the average church-goer and the righteous. When you are a churchgoer, you are more concerned about tradition, gimmicks, and the status quo; but when you are the righteous, you are concerned about experiencing something from God that you have not experienced before.

God desires to take us deeper in His Word and higher in the anointing. You can't even pray without a level of revelation. The Bible is very clear concerning prayer: *"So too the [Holy] Spirit comes to our aid and bears us up in our weakness; for we do not know what prayer to offer nor how to offer it worthily as we ought, but the Spirit Himself goes to meet our supplication and pleads in our behalf with unspeakable yearnings and groanings too deep for utterance"* (Romans 8:26, AMPC).

Revelation is a spiritual thing and cannot be obtained in your flesh. If you need spiritual revelation, you must be in the Spirit. Revelation is literally God disclosing a secret that the world is trying to figure out. Carnal men cannot comprehend the things of the Spirit. When you are carnal in nature and in spirit, you cannot understand or comprehend the realm of the Spirit. The Spirit of God is something that must be discerned by the same Spirit. If you have not been filled with the Spirit of God, then you will not be able to understand the Spirit.

It is impossible to successfully operate and function in something you cannot comprehend. Once the Kingdom of God and heaven are revealed to your Spirit, comprehension is also present. Whenever God reveals something to you by His Spirit, He also gives you the comprehension of the revelation. That is why Jesus taught the disciples and the other followers in parables – they had not yet been filled with the Spirit of God. It was important that Jesus took a heavenly story and explained it through earthly means. It is also important to understand that a mind that has not been renewed cannot comprehend Kingdom Revelation:

The Apostle Paul wrote in the book of Romans: *"I beseech you therefore, brethren, by the mercies of God, that ye present your bodies a living sacrifice, holy, acceptable unto God, which is your reasonable service. And be not conformed to this world: but be ye transformed by the renewing of your mind, that ye may prove what is that good, and acceptable, and perfect, will of God"* (Romans 12:1-2, KJV).

Something must take place in your mind in order for you to comprehend the mystic mysteries of the kingdom of God. God is concerned about the condition of my mind, because if my mind is messy than my actions will also be messy. Sometimes it is impossible for the Spirit of God to reveal or speak anything to use because we are too busy and too concerned with our daily lives. We miss so many opportunities to advance in the kingdom because the kingdom is not our priority. Let's look at the Word of God found in the tenth chapter of the book of Daniel . . . *"In the third year of Cyrus king of Persia"*, a thing *was revealed unto Daniel, whose name was called Belteshazzar; and the thing was true, but the time appointed was long: and he understood the thing, and had understanding of the vision"* (Daniel 10:1, KJV). Whenever something is revealed to you by the Spirit of God, comprehension is also available. Verses three and four follow: *"In those days, I Daniel was mourning three full weeks. I ate no pleasant bread, neither came flesh nor wine in my mouth, neither did I anoint myself at all, till three whole weeks were fulfilled."* Daniel was determined to hear from the Spirit of the Lord. Regardless of what is going on in the kingdom of this world, we must have that same desire.

In verses seven and eight (Amplified Bible, Classic Edition), Daniel declared: *"And I, Daniel, alone saw the vision [of this heavenly being], for the men who were with me did not see the vision, but a great trembling fell upon them so that they fled to hide themselves. So I was left alone and saw this great vision, and no strength was left in me, for my fresh appearance was turned to pallor; I grew weak and faint [with fright]."* Daniel was left alone when he was able to hear from the Spirit of God. It is important that your atmosphere is cleaned out when the Spirit of God is speaking. Sometimes, having too many people in your inner circle can be a hindrance because not only are you dealing with your issues, but you also have to deal with your company's issues. Let us read on in verse nine, the same Bible version: *"Then I heard the sound of his words: and when I heard the sound of his words, I fell on my face in a deep sleep, with my face [sunk] to the ground"*.

The Lord gave me a revelation, some years ago, that allows me to "sleep" whenever chaos is going on around me. When you are in the sleeping mode, you are in an unconscious state. At that point, your issues have been paused due to your earthly rest. It's important and very vital that we maintain peace while we are moving in the Kingdom. You can be at rest and going on about your daily life because you have a revelation. Despite your situation, you know by divine revelation that the Spirit of God is working on your behalf. Daniel said, in verses 10-13: *"And behold, a hand touched me, which set me [unsteadily] upon my knees and upon the palms of my hands. And [the angel] said to me, O Daniel, you greatly beloved man, understand the words that I speak to you and stand upright, for to you I am now sent. And while he was saying this word to me, I stood up trembling. Then he said to me, Fear no, Daniel from the first day that you set your mind and heart to understand and to humble yourself before your God, your words were heard, and I have come as a consequence of [and in response to] your words. But the prince of the kingdom of Persia withstood me for twenty-one days. Then*

*Michael, one of the chief [of the celestial] princes, came to help me, for I remained there with the kings of Persia"* (Daniel 10:10-13, AMPC).

The angel of the Lord was explaining to Daniel, in Daniel 10:10-13, AMPC, that although it took him a long time to get to Daniel, he was heard the very first time he prayed. In this revelation, the angel of the Lord clearly explains that although our prayers are answered, there are different demonic and hindering spirits that get in the way of our breakthrough and having our prayers answered. Although the answer is often delayed, it does not mean that it is denied. In verse 13, we see the warfare that was caused by Daniel's prayer resulted in one of the top celestial princes coming to his aid!

There is someone reading this book right now and what you are dealing with requires great assistance from the host of heaven. You must understand that our fight is not against flesh and blood. The Word clearly states: *"For we are not wrestling with flesh and blood [contending only with physical opponents], but against the despotisms, against the powers, against [the master spirits who are] the world rulers of this present darkness, against the spirit forces of wickedness in the heavenly (supernatural) sphere"* (Ephesians 6:12, AMPC). Paul lets us know in this scripture that our fight is not against anything human. What is coming against you is very spiritual, so your counterattack must also be spiritual. When we are in a spiritual fight, we must ALWAYS fight in the Spirit. We must take a stand in the Spirit, although the fiery darts are aimed at our flesh. Paul teaches us how to fight in Ephesians 6:13-17 (AMPC):

*"Therefore put on God's complete armor, that you may be able to resist and stand your ground on the evil day [of danger], and, having done all [the crisis demands], to stand [firmly in your place]. Stand therefore [hold your ground], having tightened the belt of truth around your loins and having put on the breastplate*

*of integrity and of moral rectitude and right standing with God. And having shod your feet in preparation [to face the enemy with the firm-footed stability, the promptness, and the readiness produced by the good news] of the Gospel of peace. Lift up over all the [covering] shield of saving faith, upon which you can quench all the flaming missiles of the wicked [one]. And take the helmet of salvation and the sword that the Spirit wields, which is the Word of God."*

Paul teaches us how to fight spiritually NOT carnally. The carnal mind cannot comprehend the things of the spirit. I have said this before, but you cannot operate in anything you do not comprehend or understand. The Word of the Lord says,

*"My people are destroyed for lack of knowledge: because you [the priestly nation] have rejected knowledge, I will also reject you that you shall be priest to Me; seeing you have forgotten the law of your God, I will also forget your children. The more they increased and multiplied [in prosperity and power], the more they sinned against Me; I will change their glory into shame. They feed on the sin of My people and set their heart on their iniquity. And it shall be: Like people, like priest; I will punish them for their ways and repay them for their doings* (Hosea 4:6-9, AMPC).

### HOW IS REVELATION OBTAINED?

The greatest example of a man with great revelation in the scriptures is John, the Revelator. John had so much revelation and insight on Christ, so much so that some of the disciples weren't even able to understand the intimacy between him and Christ. Revelation comes from spending intimate time with the Father. Christ knew that John was a person who could be trusted with secrets! It is like a natural relationship . . . Only someone who is unwise or unlearned would share deep intimate secrets with someone who cannot be trusted. Trust isn't something that's obtained overnight; trust is earned through suffering, tears, disappointments, and pain. It takes time to win a person's trust. When you have won a person's trust, that person does not mind being transparent with you.

Whenever there is trust in a relationship, there is a significant level of transparency. When a person becomes transparent, they began to reveal things they would not ordinarily display if they were guarded. It is very important that you are a vessel God can trust with revelation. However, everything the Lord shows you is not meant to be shared. Ordinary people will not be able to understand or comprehend some of the things the Lord will reveal. There are some spiritual things the Lord will reveal to you that are not for you to share – not even with some of your brothers and sisters in Christ. Not everyone is at a level where they can handle a particular revelation. The Apostle

Paul spoke about a revelation he received in a letter to the church at Corinth: *"True, there is nothing to be gained by it, but [as I am obliged] to boast, I will go on to visions and revelations of the Lord. I know a man in Christ who fourteen years ago—whether in the body or out of the body I do not know, God know–was caught up to the third heaven. And I know that this man–whether in the body or away from the body I do not know, God knows–was caught up into paradise, and he heard utterances beyond the power of man to put into words, which man is not permitted to utter"* (2 Corinthians 12:1-4, AMPC).

The Lord showed the Apostle Paul a great revelation about the third heaven. He made Paul privy to conversations that were being held in the heavenlies that the Apostle Paul did not speak about in this letter. Why would God share profound and personal things with the Apostle Paul? What qualified the Apostle Paul to be a partaker of such an impressive and gratifying experience? Firstly, God knew He could trust Paul! Not only did He trust Paul with secrets, but also God knew that whatever the Apostle Paul had to suffer or go through, he would do it like a good soldier. The Apostle Paul was not one to murmur and complain.

He did not become faint when God was allowing him to go through. God is looking for someone He can trust to go through the fire and to know that it is working for their good!

In 2 Timothy 2:7-12, AMPC, we see The Apostle Paul teaching his son in the gospel, Timothy: *"Think over these things I am saying [understand them and grasp their application], for the Lord will grant you full insight and understanding in everything. Constantly keep in mind Jesus Christ (the Messiah) [as] risen from the dead, [as the prophesied King] descended from David, according to the good news (the Gospel) that I preach. For that [Gospel] I am suffering affliction and wearing chains like a criminal. But the Word of God is not chained or imprisoned! Therefore I [am ready to] persevere and stand my ground with patience and endure everything for the sake of the elect [God's chosen], so that they too may obtain [the] salvation which is in Christ Jesus, with [the reward of] eternal glory. The saying is sure and worthy of confidence: If we have died with Him, we shall also live with Him. If we endure, we shall also reign with Him. If we deny and disown and reject Him, He will also deny and disown and reject us."*

Paul was teaching Timothy, by example, that to obtain the promises of God in this ministry and in the life of an actual Minister, one must be able to "go through." It is not so much what you go through but it is how you go through it! God is not looking at the fact that we are suffering; God is concerned about *how* we suffer. It's not just enough to be able to say, "I'm suffering and I'm in pain. I don't know what I'm going to do." The real testimony is that while you are suffering and while you are going through, you still have the confidence in God to declare, "But I still trust you!" "I still know you're able!" When we murmur and complain while we are suffering, we become an offence to God and He takes back a lot of the trust He has placed in us. God is looking to see if He can trust us to suffer with Him and not embarrass Him in the process.

If we do not have enough revelation to know that although we are struggling and going through hardships – God is able to bring us out – then He cannot trust us enough to open us up to more revelation.

Catch this nugget, Believer: When we suffer, it is only an opportunity for God to give us more revelation about who He is.

You will never know or believe God to be a "heart fixer" if your heart has never been broken. You will never believe God to be a "mind regulator" if you have never been at the point of losing your mind and God spoke peace in the midst of your storm. You will never believe God to be "the resurrection and the life" if you have never been at the point of death and the doctors have done all they could do. You must understand that as you suffer, God is in the process of revealing Himself to you in a close and intimate way. We learn who God is through suffering. The Apostle Paul said it best in Philippians:

*"Yes, furthermore, I count everything as loss compared to the possession of the priceless privilege (the overwhelming preciousness, the surpassing worth, and supreme advantage) of knowing Christ Jesus my Lord and of progressively becoming more deeply and intimately acquainted with Him [of perceiving and recognizing and understanding Him more fully and clearly]. For His sake I have lost everything and consider it all to be mere rubbish (refuse, dregs), in order that I may win (gain) Christ (the Anointed One), And that I may [actually] be found and known as in Him, not having any [self-achieved] righteousness that can be called my own, based on my obedience to the Law's demands (ritualistic uprightness and supposed right standing with God thus acquired), but possessing that [genuine righteousness] which comes through faith in Christ (the Anointed One), the [truly] right standing with God, which comes from God by [saving] faith. [For my determined purpose is] that I may know Him [that I may progressively become more deeply and intimately acquainted with Him, perceiving and*

*recognizing and understanding the wonders of His Person more strongly and more clearly], and that I may in the same way come to know the power outflowing from His resurrection [which it exerts over believers], and that I may so share His sufferings as to be continually transformed [in spirit into His likeness even] to His death, [in the hope] . . . "* (Philippians 3:8-10, AMPC).

It was very important to the Apostle to forsake everything for the cause of Christ! Before his conversion, Paul was a very educated man, a very well-known person in his realm. Although this brought him great success, when he had an encounter with Jesus, he forsook all of his knowledge and accomplishments to follow after Christ. Paul was a very powerful Apostle. God took him through a lot to determine if the Apostle was after His face or His hand.

Many of today's Christians have several motives for following after Christ. When God called His disciples, He required them to leave all of their belongings and follow Him. This was a way of proving their loyalty to God. He wanted to know they genuinely desired a relationship with Him without expecting anything in return. Many people never have the opportunity to receive revelation from the Father because their motives are wrong. God desires people seek after Revelation out of a relationship with Him, not as the hypocrites. Some people desire deep Revelation so they can enhance their public ministry and be more effective in their realm. The desire is birthed from wanting to be closer to the Father, but it manifests to prove a point to people. God does not want to be pimped for gifts or talents!

## Receiving manifestation

The only people receiving manifestation in this hour are those who have a relationship with God! There are steps to this process. Once you understand and comprehend the process you can go anywhere you want in the kingdom. Relationship is the first thing that you must seek. There is no Revelation without Relationship! The Father is only releasing Revelation to those who are seeking His face and not just His hand.

After a person receives Revelation, they become candidates for Manifestation. When you receive manifestation, things you did not have in the natural, but were in your Spirit, will manifest. The hand of God will demonstrate what you believed Him for! However, remember, you cannot skip the process; it is very important that we follow the steps. When you desire to purchase a house, something on the inside of you has already revealed to you that you can actually buy a house. After you have received that revelation, you move forward with the process. Anyone can purchase a home (depending upon their credit status); but it still takes a revelation to move forward with the process.

In Matthew 16:13 (AMPC), Jesus asked His disciples "Who do people say that the Son of Man is?" Jesus had not declared who He was during this season. Although He was working miracles, healing the sick, etc., He still had not come forth declaring Himself as the Christ. It was evident, when asked, that the majority of the disciples did not recognize who Jesus was because they blurted out what the crowd was saying about Him. It is very important that we understand the majority will miss it; only the remnant will really understand what the Spirit is saying. Jesus was very specific when He asked, *"But who do you (yourselves) say that I am?" Simon Peter replied, "You are the Christ, the Son of the living God." Notice how Jesus responded to Peter in verse 17: Then Jesus answered him, Blessed (happy, fortunate, and to be envied) are you, Simon Bar-Jonah. For flesh and blood (men) have not [REVEALED] this to you, but My Father Who is in heaven."*

From this reading, we understand that Peter was the only one of the disciples who clearly understood and comprehended who Christ was because he had Revelation. Because of Peter's Revelation, Christ responded to him in the eighteenth verse with these words: *"And I tell you, you are Peter [Greek, petra-a large piece of rock], and on this rock [Greek, petra-a huge rock like Gibraltar) I will build my church, and the gates of Hades (the powers of the infernal region) shall not overpower it [or be strong to its detriment or hold out against it)."*

We see that because of Peter's Revelation, Christ had something to build His house upon. When you receive Revelation, you are eligible for an upgrade in the Kingdom! This kind of miracle cannot be explained; it must be experienced. Your Kingdom Revelation gives you instant authority. Let us read on in the next verse . . . In verse 19, Jesus proclaims, *"I will give you the keys to the kingdom of heaven, and whatever you bind (declare to be improper and unlawful) on earth must be what is already bound in heaven, and whatever you loose (declare lawful) on earth must be what is already loosed in heaven."*

Most people who have no revelation find themselves in places of defeat and worry. In spite of what it looks like on the outside and despite your current condition; when you operate in Kingdom Revelation, your posture is sure. You know and recognize that because of your Revelation, you realize God has everything under control. Your revelation, however, will be tested as you begin to grow in God in faith. Let's take Peter, for instance . . . When Peter declared Jesus to be the Christ and He gave Peter the keys to the kingdom, Jesus later rebuked him because he didn't want to see Christ suffer (Matthew 16:23).

If the Lord trusts you with Revelation, your revelation must be tried and tested to ensure you are entirely convinced of who Christ is and who you are in Him. Peter was going to serve as one of the fathers of the faith. You cannot have the kind of anointing Peter carried – preaching in a room with 120 people on the day of Pentecost and the Holy Ghost visits, sitting on everyone in the room until they began to speak in other tongues – just because you made a confession of who Christ was. That kind of power sat in that room because the Apostle Peter's Revelation was TRIED and TESTED!

Peter went on trial, wrestling with His Faith, after Jesus had been captured by the Captains and the Priest. He was afraid of death, so Peter buried his revelation of who Jesus was to the point of denying Him! It's very important that during this journey, we don't judge other people. Peter was so appalled at the idea of someone betraying Jesus that he became outraged: "But Peter said unto him, Although all shall be offended, yet will not I" (Mark 14:29, KJV). *Jesus responded to his ignorance in verse 30 and said, ". . . Verily I say unto thee, That this day, even in this night, before the cock crow twice, thou shalt deny me thrice."* It is important that your revelation is tried all the way to its death! If there is no *trial* for your revelation, there can be no *victory* for your revelation. Peter's trial gained him victory on the day of Pentecost when he preached the first message to the new church. On the day of Pentecost, after the Holy Ghost fell upon them, they asked Peter and the rest of the apostles,

*" . . . Men, and brethren, what shall we do? Then Peter said unto them, Repent, and be baptized every one of you in the name of Jesus Christ for the remission of sins, and ye shall receive the gift of the Holy Ghost. For the Promise is unto you, and to your children, and to all that are afar off, even as many as the Lord our God shall call. And with many other words did he testify and exhort, saying, Save yourselves from this untoward generation. Then they that gladly received his word were baptized: and the same day there were added unto them about three thousand souls"* (Acts 2:37-41 KJV).

If Peter not had an experience with his Revelation, his convictions alone would not have been enough to release that anointing in the earth – the kind of anointing where people would receive the manifestation of the Word being made flesh. On that day of Pentecost, God recreated John 1:14: *"And the Word was made flesh, and dwelt among us, (and we beheld his glory, the glory as of the only begotten of the Father,) full of grace and truth."* The Word became flesh again because the Spirit of God came to live in our flesh, which acts as a tabernacle for the Spirit of God. To Peter, it seemed as if he did not have an authentic revelation because he had to go through the trial.

Allow me to submit to you that what is revealed does not become authoritative until it is tried! Peter had to go through the process of birthing his revelation. Your revelation, if it is truly from the Spirit of God, will come with a prophecy and a promise!

God prophesied to Peter that He was going to be the rock of the church. He also prophesied that "whatsoever he binds on earth shall be bound in heaven, and whatsoever he looses in the land shall be loosed in heaven." Both of those things came to pass in Peter's life because he went through the trial process. Your revelation by the Spirit of God is only an idea – until it is tried and tested. When you start a business, the business is only a good idea until you begin *conducting* business. It is very important that whatever is revealed to you goes into operation. If you do not follow the revelation up with action, the revelation is only a good idea.

Peter would have never been one of the great apostles had he not ran with his revelation of the Son of Man. Against all odds, Peter held to his revelation even though the One who revealed it to him looked as if it was dying. In the midst of that near death experience, Peter experienced a deeper level of confidence. He became assured that his revelation was indeed, trustworthy. The only way to find out if what you're carrying is solid is to shake the foundation that it's built upon!!!

I have said this before: Kingdom provision cannot be explained; it must be experienced. Faith must be put into action and exercised. The only way it can be exercised is by the trying of it: *"Consider it wholly joyful, my brethren, whenever you are enveloped in or encounter trials of any sort or fall into various temptations. Be assured and understand that the trial and proving of your faith bring out endurance and steadfastness and patience. But let endurance and steadfastness and patience have full play and do a thorough work, so that you may be [people] perfectly and fully developed [with no defects], lacking in nothing"* (James 1:2-4 AMPC).

The trying of your faith produces something great on the inside of you that the enemy cannot take. Examine yourself, even right now, and make sure your foundation is built upon faith. The entire basis for our salvation is based upon faith, and we can do nothing without it.

*"Now Faith is the assurance (the confirmation, the title deed) of the things [we] hope for, being the proof of things [we] do not see and the conviction of their reality [faith perceiving as real fact what is not revealed to the senses]. But without faith it is impossible to please and be satisfactory to Him. For whoever would come near to God must [necessarily] believe that God exists and that He is the rewarder of those who earnestly and diligently seek Him [out]* (Hebrews 11:1; 6, AMPC).

Begin to ask the Lord to Reveal what is hidden, ask Him to stir your Spirit so that what is dead on the inside of you will come alive.

It is my desire that after reading this book that you begin to think about what God has birthed in you. Once you discover the passion that God himself has placed on the inside of you, you can begin to pursue it. What God has *Revealed*, heaven has *Sealed*. I want you to know that *discovery* will lead to *recovery* in this season of your life.

# Biography

## Pastor & Prophet Burton Sherbert

Prophet and Pastor, Burton Sherbert, is founder of Kingdom Tabernacle of Refuge Ministries, Inc. a growing ministry located in Annapolis, Maryland. Prophet Sherbert, travels throughout the country preaching and prophesying the Word of the Lord with razor-sharp accuracy and zeal. Affectionately known as "Elijah," Dr. Annette McGuire Kenon likened him to the biblical prophet by noting, "….he has the spiritual eyes of the eagle-eyed Prophet Elijah."

As a child, Prophet Sherbert had many gifts. He played the keyboard, sung and directed the choir, but he always knew God had more for him. At the age of 15, Prophet Sherbert discerned God's call while watching Dr. Iona Locke as she preached from the Book of Samuel. Dr. Locke stated there were some Samuels in hiding and it was at that moment the Prophet Sherbert knew he was called. After his Spirit bore witness with the message of Dr. Iona Locke, Prophet Sherbert told his grandmother that he had been called to preach to which she answered "*okay*." A week later his grandmother became ill and she asked him to pray for her while she was standing in the hallway. His delayed response caused her to recant her request as she was testing him. Two weeks later his grandmother became ill again, but this time she did not have to ask for prayer because Prophet Sherbert walked into his grandmother's room and prayed for her without delay. It was at that moment that his grandmother acknowledged his calling by saying, "Whatever God has called you to do, you have my blessing."

At the age of 17, Prophet Sherbert began preaching. He received his early training at the Greater Bible Way Church under the leadership of the late Bishop Joseph N. Brown. Bishop Brown quickly noticed Burton's eagerness to learn and his musical ability so he put the young prophet's talents to use. Sherbert served in the church's music department as one of the directors of the Youth for Christ Choir. He later went on to receive his Christian education from the well-respected Washington Bible College and Capital Bible Seminary.

In the year 2000, God called Prophet Sherbert to assist in the planting of a church in Prince Frederick, Maryland. Whole Heart Deliverance Temple was a fast growing, cutting-edge ministry and Prophet Sherbert was the first Ordained Elder. He was the Praise & Worship Leader, Director of the Whole Heart Chorale, Church Administrator, and a mighty Evangelist. People would receive their deliverance before the altar call because the Word of the Lord was so rich in his belly.

With pastoral compassion and prophetic purpose, Prophet Sherbert willingly yields to the prophetic mantle placed on his life. As the Holy Spirit leads him to speak, revelatory words from God's heart are delivered to those who need edification, exhortation and comfort. This has been proven as many prophesies spoken by Prophet Sherbert have come to fruition. Wayward children have returned home, relationships have been restored, addictions delivered, successful businesses started and churches erected as a result of the Word of the Lord spoken through the prophet.

As a pastor-teacher, Prophet Sherbert brings release and revelation to many through his lively, energetic preaching style. Unassuming at first glance, Prophet Sherbert surprises church leaders and layman alike with his powerful delivery and rousing exposition of the Word. Possessing attributes of both pastor and prophet—Prophet Sherbert desires to see believers grow spiritually and desires to see the church function according to the word of the Lord. His intense love for the Lord, fearless spirit and ability to tap into the very heart of God make him a memorable speaker.

With his love for God and lively preaching style, which can hold even the skeptics attention, Pastor Sherbert speaks and shares the heart of God with compassion and conviction.

www.ingramcontent.com/pod-product-compliance
Lightning Source LLC
Chambersburg PA
CBHW051714090426
42736CB00013B/2698